The Sheep Payed For All

The Ludlows of Stokesay

By
Christopher Train

Ludlow Historical Research Group
2005

ISBN: 1874200 16 5

Published by Scenesetters
Ash-Leys, Bucknell, Shropshire, SY7 0AL
on behalf of the
Ludlow Historical Research Group
2005

Table of Contents

LIST OF ILLUSTRATIONS

AUTHOR'S PREFACE

In June 2004 the Ludlow Historical Research Group was asked by Robin Ludlow of Warminster whether a member of the Group would write a short history of the Ludlow family who had acquired the manor of Stokesay in the 1280s and built the fortified manor house there in which they and their descendants lived for some 200 hundred years. Over thirty years Robin Ludlow, himself descended from a Gloucestershire branch of the family – the Ludlows of Shipton Moyne who established themselves there in about 1470 - has been assembling documentation about those with this family name. Since numerous Ludlows across the whole country have played notable parts in their localities and nationally from the early middle ages, this is now a very substantial archive. It has been the principal source for this study of the Stokesay Ludlows. I owe an enormous debt of gratitude to Robin Ludlow for making it available to me, and also to Michael Faraday, whose collection of transcribed documents relating to the medieval history of Ludlow, copies of which are now lodged with the Ludlow Historical Research Group, is an indispensable source for anyone studying this period of Ludlow history. Due mention is made in the appropriate place of those who have made illustrations available to me. I am also grateful to Robin Ludlow and to Marion Roberts, formerly Shropshire County Archivist, for reading the text in draft. I should also acknowledge the help and encouragement I have had from David Lloyd, the Group's Director of Research, who not only asked me to undertake what has been a fascinating task, but has read the text in draft and has kept me going when I flagged. On behalf of the Group I wish to thank both Robin Ludlow and the Craven Arms History Society for giving financial assistance with the publication.

Outline pedigree of the principal members of the Ludlow family mentioned in the text

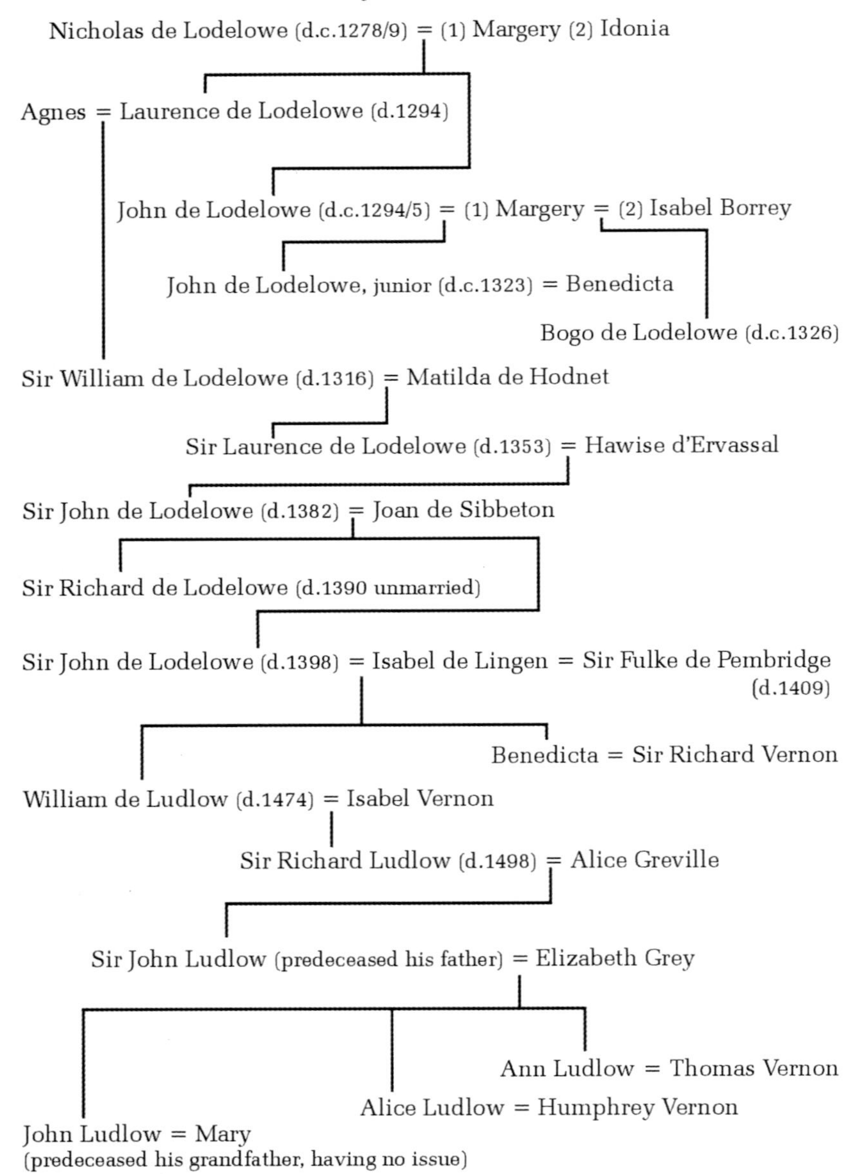

This pedigree is based largely upon one transcribed by Robin Ludlow in 2003 from a Ludlow pedigree prepared by the College of Arms, London

CHAPTER 1

'IT IS THE SHEEPE HATH PAYED FOR ALL'

On 28th October 1294 Laurence de Lodelowe, a Shropshire wool merchant, was given the protection of King Edward I to go abroad on the king's business until the following midsummer. On 12th November the king gave instructions to Laurence and his colleagues in the venture, Robert de Segre, 'receiver of the king's moneys', and Roger de Lincoln, one of the king's clerks, to pay from money raised on the wool which they were taking to Holland 4000 marks to Henry, count of Bar, and 6000 marks to the Archbishop of Cologne. This was to provide funds for the King's allies in the Low Countries and the Rhineland in his war with King Philip of France. Some days later the expedition sailed from London, but in the night of Friday 26th November a storm caught the fleet off the coast of Suffolk near Aldeburgh. Laurence de Lodelowe and Roger de Lincoln were drowned and much of the wool was lost. Laurence's body was recovered and brought back to Ludlow, to be buried in St Laurence's church there on 20th December.

Stokesay Castle and Church.

Laurence, as this story of his last days shows, was a man of national importance, like his father Nicholas de Lodelowe before him. Both had gained their wealth through dealing in wool and Laurence had used his to good advantage. Fourteen years before his death he had acquired the tenancy of Stokesay manor on the road north from Ludlow to Shrewsbury and he it was who built much of the fortified and moated manor house, Stokesay Castle now in the care of English Heritage, which survives to this day, the Great Hall and the South Tower being his creation. Together with the manors of Hodnet and Westbury, which came to William de Lodelowe, Laurence's son, on his marriage to Matilda de Hodnet, it was to be in his descendants' hands for the next two hundred years. They, though not of quite such significance nationally as Laurence and his father, were all men of wide influence and high standing in Shropshire.

So for some two hundred and fifty years, from the reign of Henry III to the reign of Henry VII, the Ludlows had their place among the most notable families in Shropshire, a status to which Stokesay Castle, their long standing home, bears witness to the present day. The story of the family is told in the chapters which follow.

CHAPTER 2

THE THIRTEENTH CENTURY CONTEXT

By the 1260s, the decade in which Nicholas de Lodelowe made his appearance on the pages of history as a Shrewsbury merchant, Ludlow, the town from which he originated, had been in existence for well over 100 years. It was a Norman foundation associated with its castle, like others in the Welsh Marches, and established by the lord of the local manor of Stanton Lacy, Walter de Lacy, who had built the castle soon after 1086. It had grown from a small settlement under the shadow of the castle walls into a thriving town of some two thousand people, with an ordered pattern of streets, a spacious market place for its weekly market, a grand church, rebuilt and extended in 1199, two schools, one a grammar school, its own well organised system of government, and a prosperous mercantile class, based mainly upon the wool industry.[1] It had now reached a point in its development and status where the presence of the castle was insufficient to provide it protection, and plans were afoot for it to be surrounded by a stone wall, which was finished by 1270.[2]

The provision of a town wall was not merely a token of the town's status. It was a response to what was a very real and continuing danger along the border with Wales during the thirteenth century. From the 1230s onwards this was the product of the territorial ambitions of the princes of Gwynedd, Llywelyn the Great and his grandson, Llywelyn ap Gruffudd, their readiness to interfere in the domestic troubles of the reign of Henry III, and the intimate involvement in those troubles of the Marcher barons, especially Roger de Mortimer of Wigmore. The immediacy of the threat for Ludlow and south Shropshire is illustrated by a number of episodes in these years. In the early 1230s Llywelyn the Great, in concert with the Earl Marshall, Richard earl of Pembroke "devastated the border far and wide, making their power felt as far as Shrewsbury". Clun and Oswestry were burnt, "the Teme Valley" devastated, and Shrewsbury taken. Again in the early 1260s there were Welsh incursions into the Marches which resulted in the capture of the castles of Bleddfa, Knucklas, Knighton, Norton and Presteigne with

Prospect of Ludlow from Whitcliffe by Vogelsanck and Lens 1722.

raiding parties penetrating as far as Eardisley and Weobley. And in 1264 Llywelyn ap Gruffudd joined forces with Simon de Montfort to secure the castles of Hereford, Hay, Ludlow and Richard's Castle. "Until the end of the thirteenth century and even beyond, military vigilance was a continuing pre-condition of lordship in the March."[3] It was Edward I's subjugation of the princes of Gwynedd in the campaigns of the late 1270s and early 1280s, the associated castle building programme in North Wales and the final violent suppression of the Welsh rebellion in 1294/5 which brought comparative security to the region's settlements. These were the circumstances in which Laurence de Lodelowe was to establish his residence at Stokesay.

Clun Castle from the west. Attacked and burnt by the Welsh in 1196. The stone castle dates from the second half of the 13th century.

Despite these periodic incursions and despite the consequent need for constant military vigilance in those who ruled the land, the border counties, especially Shropshire and Herefordshire, continued to produce the wool upon which the fortunes of many merchants, not least the de Lodelowes, were to be founded. The border sheep, ideally adapted to its poor pastures, hills and moor land, produced short wool of exceptionally fine quality, notably the wool known as the 'Lemster ore', which Professor Power called 'the golden fleece of England'.[4] England's fine wools were not just used to supply domestic cloth-makers; they were also the country's major export, particularly to the great cloth-making centres of Flanders and northern Italy. Indeed in the middle ages wool provided almost all the country's export earnings. It was also the principal source of the revenues which financed the wars of the three Edwards - in Wales, Scotland and France.

Sheep farming has remained one of the main industries of the Marches, as this picture of a great summer sheep sale at Craven Arms in the 1950s shows. Stokesay Castle lies half a mile to the south. (Photograph from Richard Blakeway.)

There were two distinct groups of wool-producers supplying this export market – on the one hand, the great abbeys and the large landowners, who had huge flocks on their demesne lands, and on the other, the commonality of small landowners and peasant farmers, with much smaller flocks but still collectively with large amounts of wool to sell into the export market. The usual practice of the former group was to contract in advance to sell their whole crop direct to the exporter, whose profit came from the difference between the price at which he bought and at which he sold abroad. In this trade foreign merchants, Flemish and then Italian, were pre-eminent, but Englishmen were present from the earliest days when records are available, and by the fourteenth century had become dominant in the market. The wool from the small producers came onto the market in a different way. Some was sold through local fairs and markets, but much was collected by middlemen for onward sale to the greater merchant exporters. Often these middlemen, the woolmongers, were burgesses of the market towns in the area of production - Ludlow and Shrewsbury offer typical examples – and they were jealous of their monopoly of the market. In 1265 Henry III granted to Shrewsbury, in gratitude for the town's support of his cause in the war against Simon de Montfort, that "no merchant should make any purchase of wool anywhere in Shropshire save in market towns of the county."[5] Frequently these middlemen dealers went on to be exporters themselves, and, we may surmise, Nicholas de Lodelowe was one of them.

CHAPTER 3

NICHOLAS DE LODELOWE

Any account of the great Shropshire mercantile family of de Lodelowe must first discuss the problems presented by the early medieval use of surnames. Locative surnames constitute the largest proportion of surnames in both town and country which have been analysed in the early middle ages; these are surnames which give the place of the person's origin or, less commonly, identify a lord of a particular manor. They were used to identify someone who had moved into the locality from elsewhere, as opposed to surnames of relationship, more common in the country than the town, surnames of occupation, more common in town than country, and nicknames. Family names were introduced into England by the Norman barons and, being useful for record in public documents by officials and lawyers, gradually spread to lesser landowners and then to people who had no land at all. But for a long time a surname might lapse in the next generation, so the process of producing hereditary family names for everyone was protracted, becoming more common as the thirteenth century progressed, but lasting in some parts of the country for some three hundred years from the Conquest.[6]

In the case of the surname de Lodelowe (de Ludelawe or Lodelawe are frequent variants)[7] there is no certainty that people called this were related; indeed, unless there is some other indication, for example a common father's or a brother's or wife's name or a linking context, the preferable assumption is that they were not. The Registers of Thomas de Cantilupe, Bishop of Hereford from 1275 to 1282 illustrate the point. In the Ordination List of 18th September 1277 at Leominster 45 subdeacons are named, the great majority with locative surnames. Of these three carry the surname de Lodelawe –William son of Philip, Philip, and Master Nicholas, and there is also mentioned Master William de Lodelawe. The first William named may be the son of the second person named – one cannot be sure – but the relationship, if any, of the others to each other must be unknown, all that can be said is that they came from Ludlow Three years later Brother Philip was ordained deacon at Ledbury, a reasonable supposition, but no more, being that he was the Philip ordained subdeacon in 1277. A Master William de Lodelawe appears in a number of other places in the Registers, as Official of the Archdeacon of Hereford in 1277 and as Proctor in the Roman Courts in 1280, and may very well be the same man as is mentioned in the Ordination List.[8] Whether any of these men were connected to the mercantile family cannot be said.

The story of that family begins, certainly, in 1261. The accounts of the Bailiffs of Shrewsbury for that year record that Nicholas de Lodelowe had taken 101 sacks of wool through the town gate by the Abbey and 22 sacks through the Castle Gate in the last week of June – that is some 30,000 fleeces.[9] By 1272 Nicholas de Lodelowe (in this context surely the same man) is described in the Patent Rolls as merchant of Edward, the king's son, and in 1275 as the king's merchant; in this period he is regularly referred to as a merchant of Shrewsbury.[10] So a merchant from the provinces reached national eminence. How had this happened and where had he come from? The answers to both of these questions are shrouded in obscurity.

So far as his origins are concerned, the most that can be said with any certainty is that he originated from Ludlow and that his family retained strong connections there. The earliest references to a member of the family, Laurence de Lodelowe, having property in the town date from the 1280s, but Laurence is named as a witness of legal transactions there in the 1270s.[11] The fullest account of a family property is in a Ludlow Palmers' Gild title deed, dated 25th July 1296: "I, Master Roger de Lodelawe, son of Nicholas de Lodelawe, merchant, once rector of Chalgrove, Oxfordshire, have granted for ever to Agnes, daughter of the said Nicholas, my sister, ...all my rights... in all that messuage with appurtenances which is situated in Mullestrete in the town of Lodelowe between the lane and the messuage which Geoffrey Caretarius once held..." One of the witnesses was Thomas de Lodelawe, "my brother".[12] The family's property holding in various parts of the town continued, as will emerge, for nearly three hundred years.

It is to be presumed that Nicholas acquired his surname (if it was not inherited – but no references to his forebears have been found) when he moved away from Ludlow, perhaps to establish himself and his business in Shrewsbury, which was the principal focus of the

Mill Street, Ludlow, where the de Lodelowes had property in the thirteenth century. (A nineteenth century photograph from David Lloyd.)

wool trade in western England. A reference after his death called him a burgess of Shrewsbury.[13] The Shrewsbury Merchants' Gild Roll of 1252 has the name Nicholas de Lodelawe, but it has been struck out.[14] The reason for the erasure cannot be known, but the existence of the name does suggest his presence in Shrewsbury as a merchant by this date. His name does not appear in the Roll of 1239. Too much weight cannot be put upon this negative evidence, but it is reasonable to suppose that Nicholas came to Shrewsbury in the 1240s and built his business over the next fifteen or so years until he was one of the leading wool merchants in the land. Further, archaeological and archival research have combined to suggest the possible identity of Nicholas' house in the town, on the corner of Pride Hill and Roushill Lane, the site on part of which stood a property known as Bennett's Hall. Summing up this evidence in 2000, W. A. Champion wrote, "Given the obvious commercial significance of the site at perhaps the most important crossing in the town, and the exceptional quality of some of the recorded carving...., it is at least plausible that the site was acquired by a Ludlow soon after 1254, with a magnificent town house shortly afterwards being erected on the spot. If so, it would almost certainly have been built by Nicholas Ludlow...."[15]

Nicholas' reputation as the greatest wool merchant of the day derives from the part he played in the troubles with Flanders in the 1270s. In the second half of the thirteenth century the Flemish towns of Bruges and Ghent, in what is now south west Belgium, and Ypres, in north west France, were the great centres of the cloth-making industry in northern Europe. As such they were one of the principal outlets for English wool, with their merchants and English merchants active in reciprocal trade. In 1270, not for the first time, Margaret, countess of Flanders, in retaliation for the non-payment of a pension which was due to her from Henry III, seized the goods of foreign merchants and expelled them from Flanders. The English Crown immediately responded similarly and placed an embargo on the export of wool to Flanders. One of the consequences of these events was the creation in England of a licensing system for wool exports, together with the imposition of strict controls on mercantile activity. It is this system, with its associated records, which enables a picture to be drawn of the English wool export trade in the 1270s and of the part which Shrewsbury merchants, and particularly Nicholas de Lodelowe, played in it.[16]

The Burg in Bruges - the old centre of the town - taken from the Belfry. The Town Hall (1376-1400) is on the right. (Photograph by David Jones.)

In 1273 just over a quarter of the wool exported was by English merchants. Between 1271 and 1274 327 English merchants were licensed, of whom 96 were London based, 40 from Winchester, 19 from Southampton, 15 from Andover and Newcastle, and 12 and 6 respectively from Shrewsbury and Ludlow. The great majority of towns had only a handful of merchants. In the Marches Hereford and Chester had only 1 each and Abergavenny 2. The predominance of Shrewsbury and Ludlow in the area is manifest. Among the Shrewsbury merchants Nicholas stands out. In the seizures of 1270 he had lost 330 sacks to the value of £1,828 11s 5d, and in 1273 he was licensed to export up to 300 sacks; comparable figures for another considerable Shrewsbury merchant (Roger Pride) for these years were 32 sacks valued at £203 8s 4d and a licence to export 120 sacks. William Randolf and Richard Barri (Borrey), both of Shrewsbury, were each licensed for 20 sacks. In 1274 Nicholas, his sons, Laurence and John, and Richard Borrey were all licensed to export wool (without specification of amount) but not to Flanders. In May 1277 Nicholas, explicitly the king's merchant, was licensed to export 250 sacks, Laurence 200 sacks and Richard Pride 200 sacks (these were the largest amounts of any English merchant, although matched by some syndicates of Italian merchants). Nicholas' dealings in Flanders are also revealed by the King's order in 1279 to the mayor of Ypres, made on behalf of Nicholas' executors after his death "who have power to sue for, levy and receive all his debts and chattels wherever they may be", to deliver the goods "late of the said Nicholas" to his executors.[17]

But the most significant indication of Nicholas' national and international standing is that, when in 1274 Edward I agreed with Guy of Flanders, son of countess Margaret, terms for the reparation of the damages arising from the 1270 seizures to the tune of £4,755 and when the Flemings dragged their heels over payment, in 1276 "The king being determined to endure it no longer has appointed Nicholas de Ludelowe and Thomas de Basingges as his special proctors to demand and receive the said sum." In November 1277 there was money still owing, but a sum of £2,022 had been "already paid by the hands of Nicholas de Lodelawe by the merchants of Ypre, Doway, Popering and Dykemue as their contingent of the debt to the English merchants."[18]

Nicholas dealt in huge numbers of fleeces – there were some 240 fleeces to the sack. Where did it come from? Clearly from the top class sheep of the Welsh borderland, but there is no certain evidence of local sources. His part in a dispute in the 1270s between the men of Montgomery and the burgesses and merchants of Shrewsbury and Ludlow points to his involvement in the wool trade in this part of the Marches. The former complained about a market which had been established at Welshpool by the lord of Powys "at the instance of Nicholas de Lodelowe and of Alan Kec and other burgesses"; they tried, but failed, to get the Shropshire merchants barred from trading in their own town.[19] It is also tempting to think that the licence granted to him and Fulk de Buildwas in June 1272 indicates that they were partners handling the wool from the Cistercian Abbey of Buildwas.[20] Cistercians "were not the first monastic sheep farmers, but they turned it into an art form".[21] There is also one indication that he dealt further afield. Upon his death, the abbot of Bruerne Abbey in Oxfordshire, another Cistercian foundation, in 1286 admitted that the abbey owed 2,173 marks (about £1,450) and £103 to his heirs, his sons, Laurence, John and Thomas "begotten on

Buildwas Abbey, Shropshire. A Cistercian Abbey from 1147. The Cistercians were major producers of wool in the Middle Ages.

Margery, his late wife."[22] In 1289 the debt was still unpaid, being recorded as 2,000 marks and "five sacks of wool, price 100 marks, to wit 20 marks each sack." This suggests that Nicholas had had a contract with the Abbey, perhaps for some 100 sacks, which was not fulfilled by the time of his death.

Although it was to be Laurence de Lodelowe who firmly established the family in the ranks of the landed gentry, there is some evidence that he may have been following in his father's footsteps. In a law suit in 1267 a Nicholas de Lodelawe and his wife, Margery, claimed land in the manor of Yarkhill; there is a Yarkhill south east of Leominster and the name of his wife makes it plausible to assume that this was the merchant Nicholas de Lodelowe – and the family held land in various parts of Herefordshire later. And after his death Laurence as his executor, claimed arrears of rent from the vicar and other inhabitants of Shawbury in mid-Shropshire, which points to Nicholas having had property there.[23]

Nicholas died sometime between February 1278, when the Flemish burgesses and merchants were ordered by the king to pay moneys "by the hands of Nicholas de Lodelowe, the king's merchant, one of the attorneys of the English merchants" and August 1279, by which time his executors were administering his estate. Margery, by whom he had had his family, pre-deceased him, his widow by that time being named as Idonia.[24]

He had had a career of great distinction and success and he left a considerable heritage, but where he had come from and how he had gained his start the historical record does not reveal. There was a Thomas de Lodelawe in the Shrewsbury Gild of Merchants in 1232[25], but there is no saying whether he and Nicholas were related and even if they were that takes one no further back than the next previous generation. Recent DNA testing of some people with the Ludlow name shows that they are probably of Celtic stock from the Welsh borders, but as yet no link has been established between the modern Ludlows and Nicholas' line. If Nicholas' predecessors in Ludlow were there when the Normans came, it is possible that they used a position with the lords of Ludlow, the Lacys, to set them on the road to success. It is equally possible that Nicholas, like so many successful businessmen through the ages, used his native wit, his energy and his business acumen to set himself on the road to success.

CHAPTER 4

THE NEXT GENERATION

LAURENCE, JOHN AND THOMAS DE LODELOWE

Nicholas had at least six children – four sons, Laurence (probably the eldest, since he appears first on the list of Nicholas' executors), John, Thomas, Roger - and two daughters, Agnes and Cecily. Cecily moved away, marrying John Adrien, a rich London draper; Agnes remained unmarried, at one point living in Mill Street in Ludlow.[26] Roger, as has already been mentioned, was a priest, being at one time rector of Chalgrove in Oxfordshire. It is possible that he was in the 1270s rector of Onibury, just north of Ludlow, but there is no certain connection between that Roger and the merchant family.[27] The other three brothers followed in their father's footsteps as wool merchants.

John and Thomas may be dealt with first and briefly since the Shropshire line did not descend through them. John, described as merchant and burgess of Shrewsbury, was one of the great men of the town, being a theynesman (that is, one of the governors) of the Merchants' Gild, together with Roger Pride and Richard Borrey, other leading wool merchants of the day, in 1281.[28] In or about 1283 – his son, Bogo de Lodelowe, by this, his second marriage, was 12 in 1295 - he married Isabel Borrey, the widow of Richard Borrey, and together soon after they received, through the gift of Sir John Lestrange, a moiety (half) of the manor of Chipping Campden in Cotswold wool country. The inquisition *post mortem* on John's death is dated 8th August 1295.[29] He was buried in Chipping Campden church and, although Isabel returned to Shrewsbury and resumed the name of her first husband, the manor, through his son Bogo de Lodelowe, remained in the hands of the Campden de Lodelowes until the early fifteenth century.[30] Thomas was also described as merchant in the wool trade in the 1270s. He married Joan, the youngest daughter and co-heiress of Sir Philip Marmion, the King's Champion, a title which her husband inherited in due course. His wife brought with her property in the Lincolnshire Wolds (wool country again) and in

Surrey, at Walton, Tooting and Mitcham. He was made Knight of the Bath in 1306 on the occasion of the knighting of Edward, Prince of Wales and subsequently a knight of Surrey. He died in 1313 and his male line did not extend beyond the next generation.[31]

Laurence stayed with his Shropshire roots, indeed with his Ludlow roots. For, unlike his father, who, in the light of the absence of substantive reference to him in that town's records, seems to have been little involved in its affairs, he was frequently in Ludlow. His name occurs as witness to legal transactions from 1271/2 onwards into the 1290s. He acquired houses and shops in the town during the 1280s.[32] He was involved in the government of the town; the Ludlow account Rolls of 1288 show him, with four others (two of whom were certainly local wool merchants), as responsible for the collection (the 'farm') of the demesne rents of Theobald de Verdun's half of the town; for this they "paid annually 10 marks whereof they found securities", Laurence himself paying 2 marks.[33] And in a lawsuit of 1278 for alleged misappropriation of goods Laurence's name is joined as co-defendant with fifteen others, among them some of the most notable members of the Ludlow community at the time,

The Bull Ring, Ludlow, looking into The Narrows.
The de Lodelowes had property here from the thirteenth century.
(An early 20th century photograph from David Lloyd.)

notably Geoffrey Andrew, the first warden of the Palmers' Gild, William Pygin, one of the town's bailiffs in 1272, and members of the Agace, Eylrich and Piwau families.[34] On a more sombre and ominous note, in view of the violence which was to trouble the family in later years, in 1290 William Piers of Brompton lodged a complaint that various named people in Ludlow "together with the commonality of the town of Ludlow, whose names are unknown save that of Laurence of Ludlow, came and suddenly attacked him, wounded him, and stripped him and threw him into prison."[35] From all of this it may be surmised that Laurence made Ludlow, rather than Shrewsbury, the base of his business and his home until he acquired Stokesay.

Little evidence survives about the extent of Laurence's trade in the export of wool, one licence given in 1277 was for 200 sacks at the same time as his father was licensed for 250.[36] But Laurence traded also in cloth.[37] And, perhaps as important for the foundation of his fortune, he, like many other great merchants (not least the Italians who were the leading bankers of this period), provided finance for the wool trade, advancing credit and actual loans to fellow merchants and to landlords. Discussing the involvement of Shrewsbury merchants in the financing of the wool trade, the Cromartys in *The Wealth of Shrewsbury in the Early Fourteenth Century* cited the number of default suits in which Shrewsbury merchants were involved: "...between 1300 and 1312 John Gamel was trying to retrieve debts of £140 in fourteen separate actions; Richard Stury initiated twenty three actions between 1291 and 1306, amounting to £94.15.11d. Between 1285 and 1305 William Vaughan tried to regain an even larger sum, £223.12s in sixteen cases..."[38] These were very substantial sums and those involved were among the wealthiest men in one of England's largest towns at the time. Over the period 1281 until his death in 1294 Laurence de Lodelowe is recorded as having undertaken fourteen actions to recover moneys owed to him - to the value of £800. Amongst his debtors were Theobald de Verdun, joint lord of Ludlow (£40), Edmund Mortimer of Wigmore (£321), Roger Mortimer of Wigmore (£77), and Richard, earl of Arundel (£105), and after his death his executors sued Thomas Corbet for £1,000.[39] These are among the greatest names in the Welsh Marches. But beyond that he was recorded as having lent 1,000 marks for the "king's service" in 1290 and a loan of £100 to the king was outstanding on his death.[40] When these sums are compared with those lent by the wealthiest of the great Shrewsbury merchants and when the status of those to whom the money was lent is taken into account, Laurence's reputation as one of the most famous merchants of his day can be seen to be well founded.

But commercial wealth was always vulnerable, so it is not surprising to find Laurence beginning to invest in property. That brought not only greater security but also the greater status of landed gentry. In addition to his Ludlow properties, he had land in Cold Weston and Wheathill, both on the flanks of Brown Clee Hill in Shropshire,[41] and in Overton, just to the south of Ludlow, and an estate in Much Marcle in Herefordshire, which included a water mill.[42] More important for his place in the history of Shropshire and its place in the heritage of England, in 1281 he acquired by the gift of John de Grey and his wife Maud, for the price of a 'juvenile sparrow hawk' and the payment of 8d. annually on 24th June, the tenancy of the manor of Stokesay, John de Grey holding it from Theobald de Verdun, joint lord of Ludlow.[43] Later in 1281 royal warrant bestowed upon Laurence free warren (hunting rights for small game) in all his demesne lands in Stokesay and nearby Newton and Whettleton.[44] Possession of the manor brought with it the feudal duty, since it was ultimately held from the king, of a 'knight's fee', that is the requirement, in time of war, to give service to the Crown, in this case 40 days at Montgomery Castle. Despite this chain of obligations, Laurence, as the lord of the manor, was in a position and had the means to develop the property.

The North Tower, Stokesay Castle, substantially rebuilt by Laurence de Lodelowe in the 1280s.

There was undoubtedly a manor house on the site of what is now Stokesay Castle when Laurence acquired it, parts of the North Tower being dated on the evidence of its stonework as early to mid-thirteenth century and woodwork in the solar block being dendro-dated to the 1260s. However the building which now stands on the site, apart from the Gatehouse, was Laurence's creation in the 1280s. The North Tower was substantially rebuilt (dendro-dates of 1287 and 1290), the Great Hall was built (dendro-date 1284-5), perhaps to replace an earlier timber structure, the solar wing was re-roofed (dendro-date 1289), and finally the fortified South Tower was constructed and the whole was surrounded by a castellated wall after 1291. For it was in that year that Laurence obtained royal permission "to strengthen his dwelling house of Stok [sic] Say, co. Salop, with a wall of stone and lime, and to crenellate the same."[45] The wall has now gone, destroyed in the Civil War, and the Gatehouse dates from the seventeenth century, but it is still possible to recognise the quality of the house which Laurence built for himself, one that befitted his status as a great merchant and a man of national importance, while falling short of the grand castles which were the homes of the longer standing aristocracy.

The South Tower at Stokesay Castle from the moat, showing part of the fortifications created by Laurence de Lodelowe c.1291.

Stokesay was a fortified manor house – it was only much later that it came to be called a castle – providing a spacious and comfortable home for its owner, yet having defensive characteristics which not only signified the status of its builder but were still very necessary in this border country. As has already been remarked, the Edwardian conquest of Wales was still in hand when Laurence acquired Stokesay, and in the year of his death a last and desperate rebellion, which was savagely put down, indicated that peaceful times could not yet be entirely guaranteed. In 1306 a number of south Shropshire vills, including Peaton, Burwarton and Horderley – the first and the last within five miles of Stokesay - sought relief from their taxes because they had been "burnt and plundered, and destroyed by the Welsh."[46] Stokesay would not have withstood a prolonged siege, but its defences were quite sufficient to hold off casual marauders.

Its location made it a highly convenient residence for a wool merchant of local and national standing. It stood on the north/south road which linked the two principal wool towns of the Marches – Ludlow and Shrewsbury. It lay no more than a mile away from the road which in earlier days had been the principal route between Shrewsbury and Hereford (in these parts on the line of the old Roman road, the Watling Street West) and which passed the abbey of Wigmore and the castle there, still the seat of the great Marcher lords, the Mortimers, with whom Laurence had substantial business connections. And a number of the drovers' roads out of Wales and the Marches and on into the Midlands of England passed close by.

Laurence's importance on the national stage is demonstrated most clearly by his involvement in the events which were to lead eventually to his death. Edward I had inherited huge debts from his father and from the late 1270s his efforts to subdue Wales, with the consequent substantial castle building programme, were a heavy drain on the exchequer. At the same time the king, as duke of Aquitane, was committed, under increasing pressure from King Philip of France, to maintaining his hold on Gascony, his sole remaining French territory. Incursions by the French had to be repulsed and expeditions sent, all placing further demands upon the national purse. Lay subsidies – that is taxes raised on moveable property – in 1275 and 1283 went some way to meeting these demands. However, when in the early 1290s Edward, in order to strengthen his position against the French king, sought alliances with and assistance from the princes of the Netherlands and the Rhineland, more money was urgently required. So in 1294 he turned to the wool trade to supply the necessary revenue.

In June plans were made and orders issued for all stocks of wool greater than half a sack to be seized by royal agents (a so-called 'prise'), but in the face of resistance from, and as a result of negotiations with, the leading merchants, the prise was abandoned and in its place a tax of three marks (40 shillings), the maltote or 'evil tax', was to be levied on each sack of wool exported, a six-fold increase in the customs duty. So far as the merchants were concerned, some of this burden would, no doubt, have been relieved by an increase in the price at the point of sale, but it was, for all that, a heavy imposition. Laurence de Lodelowe had the leading part in the negotiations which persuaded the merchants, reluctantly in some cases, to concede the maltote. Reporting his death the Dunstable Annalist, not an altogether disinterested witness, since Dunstable was a major wool centre, said "It was he who induced the merchants of England to concede to the king forty shillings for each sack of wool...And because he sinned against the wool merchants, he was engulfed by the waves in a ship loaded with wool."[47] Nonetheless Laurence's part in these events indicates his standing among his undoubtedly hard-nosed business contemporaries and at the same time the king's confidence in him.

On 26th July preparations began for an expedition to the Low Countries which would enable the king to gain immediate benefit from the new export tax on wool and so to subsidise his allies there. A consortium of leading merchants led by Laurence entered into an agreement with the Crown which had three elements: the merchants were to pay the custom duty on the wool they were exporting to royal officials abroad; they undertook to lend the king part of the proceeds on the wool sold abroad; and Laurence himself agreed to sell wool which the Crown had confiscated from Italian merchants. He was to be in charge of the expedition together with Master Roger de Lincoln, a royal clerk. On 28th October a letter of protection "until Midsummer, for Laurence de Lodelowe, going overseas" was issued, and on 12th November, with the fleet ready to sail, instructions were issued to "Laurence de Lodelowe, Robert de Segre, and Roger de Lincoln to pay out of the first money arising from the wool that the king lately ordered to be taken by them from his realm to Holland, to Henry, count of Bar, 4,000 marks, in part payment of a sum of money which the king is bound to him by certain agreements made between them."[48] They received an identical order to pay 6,000 marks to the Archbishop of Cologne. The wool fleet sailed from London but on Monday 29th November news reached London that the ship in which Laurence and Roger de Lincoln were sailing had been wrecked in a storm "between the night and the day" on the previous Friday with the loss of their lives; the wool it was carrying and other goods belonging to the king were thrown up on the shore near Aldeburgh, to be purloined by the locals.[49] Laurence's body was recovered and taken back to Ludlow, where he was buried on 20th December.[50]

So Laurence, as a petition in March 1295 by his widow, Agnes, put it, "paid the debt of nature on the king's service".[51] He had consolidated and extended the business which his father, Nicholas, had bequeathed him; he had established himself as one of the king's most trusted and nationally influential merchants; he had laid the foundations for his family's future as substantial Shropshire landed gentry; and, almost above all, he had created the fortified manor house, Stokesay Castle, which, by good fortune, survives to this day as "altogether...one of the most perfect and interesting thirteenth century buildings which we possess."[52]

The western aspect of Stokesay Castle with the Great Hall in the centre of the range.

CHAPTER 5

THE EARLY FOURTEENTH CENTURY

Laurence's widow, Agnes, continued his business on his death, she, his son William and Thomas de Lodelowe being his executors.[53] However, William's importance in the family's history lies not in his role in the wool trade but in his development of the second legacy which Laurence had bequeathed him – his position as one of the landed gentry in the border counties. For he made a very advantageous marriage, to Matilda de Hodnet, the daughter and heiress of William de Hodnet.

The Hundred House at the centre of Hodnet with the church behind.

The de Hodnet family took their name from the village of that name which lies six miles south west of Market Drayton on the way to Shrewsbury. The de Hodnets were the hereditary seneschals of Montgomery Castle, whose duties, listed at the time of the death of Odo de Hodnet in 1284, were that "he should abide in the Bailiwick of Montgomery Castle at the charges and discretion of its lords [that is, when duty required it], and should have a house there sufficient

Montgomery Castle. The de Lodelowes were seneschals here from 1300.

for himself, his wife and one damsel, and the rest of his following. If he tarried there for his own pleasure, he was to pay his own charges. When on duty he might have 5 horses, 4 greyhounds and 6 brachets (setters) in his train."[54] This service brought with it the lordship of the manor of Hodnet, which included a number of townships in the district southwards from Hodnet towards what is now Telford – Peplow, Bolas, Preston upon Weald Moors, and Horton – two mills, the profits of the Manor Court, and a weekly market. The de Hodnets also held land in Westbury, to the west of Shrewsbury, Welbatch in Annscroft, immediately to the south of Shrewsbury, and Moston in Stanton upon Hine Heath, in Hodnet Hundred but not part of the Hodnet manor, both of the latter being held from Fulk Fitz Warin. When Matilda de Hodnet married William de Lodelowe, sometime around 1300, he became joint holder with his wife of all these properties, in addition to the lands and properties he had inherited from his father at Stokesay, in Ludlow, and at Much Marcle.[55] In 1293 he, or perhaps his father, Laurence – the record is unclear – had acquired Rowton and Ellerdine, which he held from Fulk Lestrange; these are also close to Hodnet but not in the manor. All this not only secured his fortune and gave him substantial revenues, it also brought with it notable duties and obligations which were the marks of his status.

Westbury Church. The de Lodelowes had property in the manor and the advowson of the church from 1300.

He was summoned "in person with horses and with arms" to service overseas in France mustering at London in July 1297 and in Scotland mustering at Berwick in June 1301, by virtue of his knight's holdings in Herefordshire. In 1314 he was called to join arms in Edward II's expedition to Scotland which ended with the disastrous rout at Bannockburn, although whether William de Lodelowe was on the field there is not recorded. He was again summoned to serve in Scotland in 1316, but seems to have been excused because of ill health.[56] He was appointed a commissioner of the peace in Shropshire on five occasions between 1307 and 1314, on each occasion together with Richard de Harley. The commission of December 1307 gives an account of the duties: "To be keepers of the peace for that county during the king's absence beyond the seas, to make proclamations throughout the county that the king's peace and the statute of Winchester are to be observed inviolate, to take all necessary precautions and to announce that the currency is to be of the same weight and value, and that no wares or merchandizes are to be sold at a higher price than their true value in the time of the late king. They are empowered to appoint two burgesses in each borough and two lawful men in each market town to enforce the observation of the above regulations. They are to attach all breakers of these ordinances, rebels and forestallers, and to detain them in custody."[57] In 1302 the king appointed him along with two others to collect the lay subsidy of one fifteenth to be taken on all moveable goods for the County of Herefordshire, and he had this duty in Shropshire in 1307, 1309, 1314, 1315 and 1316.[58] Finally in this roll of duties, in 1311, 1314 and 1315 he was appointed supervisor of the array of arms for Shropshire, with the duty to enforce attendance and report defaulters to the king.[59]

His standing was, like that of his uncle, Thomas de Lodelowe, also marked by his creation as Knight of the Bath on the occasion of the knighting of Edward Prince of Wales in May 1306, and by his attendance at the Parliament of 1307 as a knight of the shire.[60]

A very different set of circumstances confirms his position as a significant name in the ranks of the Shropshire gentry. In the years following Edward II's accession in 1307 the new king and his ambitious favourite, Piers Gaveston, were confronted by the great magnates of the land, led by Thomas, earl of Lancaster, the king's cousin, who were seeking to restrain the powers of the crown which Edward I had wielded oppressively to raise money and materials for his wars against Wales, France and Scotland. In 1311 ordinances limiting the king's powers were promulgated in Parliament and Gaveston was exiled. His return at the instance of the king was virtually a declaration of civil war and the Ordinancers, as the great magnates were called, took up arms against the king and his favourite. Gaveston was captured and on 19th June 1312 put to death by the earls of Lancaster, Hereford and Arundel. There were bitter disputes over the next year about the legality of this act, until finally in October 1313 the earls consented to make a public apology and in return the king pardoned them and their adherents. "Pardon to Thomas, earl of Lancaster, and his adherents, followers and confederates, of all causes of anger, indignation, suits, accusations arisen in any manner on account of Peter de Gaveston, from the time of the king's marriage with his dear companion Isabella, whether on account of the capture, detention, or death of Peter de Gaveston, or on account of any forcible entries into any towns or castles or any sieges of the same; or on account of having borne arms, or of having taken any prisoners, or of having entered into any confederacies whatever, or in any other manner touching or concerning Peter de Gaveston, or that which befell him....The like, word for word, to the under mentioned persons adherents of Thomas, earl of Lancaster, for the death of Peter de Gaveston".[61] There follow some 500 names, beginning with Humphrey de Bohun, earl of Hereford and Essex, and Guy de Beauchamp, earl of Warwick, and including William de Lodelowe together with other Shropshire gentry with whom he had a connection, the Lestranges and Fitz Warins. William did not, however, live to see the Civil War of 1321/2, which culminated in the king's defeat of his opponents at the Battle of Boroughbridge and the execution of Thomas of Lancaster.

One other recorded episode in his life remains to be told. This takes the story back to the Shrewsbury de Lodelowes and the years immediately following the deaths of Laurence and John de Lodelowe senior, although its consequences were not finally resolved until ten years after William's death in 1316.

One of the wealthiest and most influential men in Shrewsbury for the next twenty five years or so after 1294 was John de Lodelowe junior. Historians have always called this man the son of John de Lodelowe, son of Nicholas. If he was - and this seems likely, given his wealth and his standing in the wool trade -, he was one of the sons of John's first marriage to Margery[62] (another son, Laurence, was one of John de Lodelowe senior's executors).[63] John junior emerges from the taxation records of the first decade of the fourteenth century, in terms of his moveable goods, as a very rich man, of comparable wealth to the wealthiest provincial merchants in prosperous towns elsewhere;[64] in 1309, for example, his goods were valued at £52 10s., the next highest valuations being those of William Vaughan and Richard Stury, two of the great Shrewsbury names, at £33 6s. 8d.[65] He was bailiff in 1294/5, and Burgess of the Parliament in 1301 and 1313; and was the most senior theynesman of the Merchants' Gild in 1318/19, being joined on the list of town merchants by four sons, Roger, William, Thomas and another John. Like Agnes, Laurence's widow, John junior continued active in the wool trade, the records for 1297/8 showing him to have exported 199 sacks in that year.[66] And it seems likely that he was the John de

Lodelowe, referred to as the king's merchant, "whose goods and merchandise were wrongfully taken in the land of the duke of Brabant a long time ago" and in whose interests and in those of other merchants who were creditors of the duke of Brabant the king intervened in 1302.[67] He may also, like his uncle, Laurence, have lent money to the king.[68] He was dead by 1324/5, since in that year there was an exchange of a property in Shrewsbury between his widow, Benedicta, and his son Thomas.[69]

The de Lodelowes, then, maintained a substantial presence in Shrewsbury in the persons of John junior and his family.[70] Sir William de Lodelowe, on the other hand, was involved rather in the affairs of the county than of the town, although he did become embroiled in the events which were a cause célèbre in Shrewsbury for some years after 1303. In September of that year under the leadership of Isabel Borrey (John de Lodelowe senior's widow who had reverted to the name of her first husband) and Robert de Bucknell, a group of twenty four conspirators, some townsmen, including Isabel's three Borrey sons by her first husband, together with a number of county gentry, forcibly removed the elected bailiffs, William Vaughan and John Gamel, substituted their own men and took control of the government of the town "intimidating the inhabitants from trading within the town and outside it". At the beginning of October, with Richard Stury in the lead, the town's principal burgesses counter-attacked. A large crowd broke into Isabel's house and in the ensuing melee one man was killed and two others wounded. The rightful bailiffs were restored to office, but the matter did not end there. A series of court cases lasting into 1307 ensued, with the principal issues being tried before the so-called Trailbaston courts. These were created by Edward I in face of grave concern about the breakdown of law and order in the country in the 1290s – 'trailbaston' meant one who carried a cudgel and so came to be used to describe a class of violent criminals who "as brigands and hired ruffians bludgeoned, maltreated and robbed the king's lieges during his absence or absorption in foreign wars";[71] thence it was applied to the ordinances, justices and courts which were established in 1304-5 to deal with them and, more generally, to try cases of criminal conspiracy.

The complicated, tortuous and often confusing details of these trials in Shrewsbury and the events preceding and surrounding them are not central to this story, other than that Sir William de Lodelowe was caught up in them. One of Richard Stury's allies in the county was Richard de Harley. He together with three other men, one of whom was William de Lodelowe, were in November 1305 convicted of conspiracy; in Harley's case some of the charges related to his time as sheriff, an office from which he had been removed "as not a sufficient person", but others were connected to the factional disputes within the town. Harley was fined £200 and William £100. As has been seen, this conviction does not seem to have damaged either Harley's or William's career in the subsequent administration of justice in the county.[72]

Two other points should be made about this affair. First, a William de Lodelowe was named by Isabel Borrey as one of the 72 men who attacked her premises, "broke her gates and houses there, carried away her goods and beat and maimed her servants". This could have been Sir William – there were other distinguished citizens and merchants among the attackers (Richard Stury, William Vaughan and John Gamel were named at their head), but William de Lodelowe's name comes far down the list and it could be that this William was another man. Other contemporary references suggest that this was so. The taxation records of 1306 and 1309 have a William de Lodelowe, whose means were then modest[73] (this might of course reflect the fact that Sir William retained a small property in Shrewsbury for use when he visited), and a William de Lodelowe appears in a list of Shrewsbury burgesses of 1312.[74] Again this could be Sir William, but he is nowhere else described as a burgess of Shrewsbury. Finally a William de Lodelowe was the subject of a criminal investigation for assault in Shrewsbury in late 1315.[75] Once more this could have been Sir William, but it was within months of his death (the Inquisition *post mortem* on his death was dated 11th October 1316) and, as noted above, Weyman believed him to be in ill health in the last year of his life.[76] A more plausible supposition is that this and the other references to William de Lodelowe were to the son of John junior mentioned earlier. Certainly the William de Lodelowe who was one of Shrewsbury's Burgesses of the Parliament in 1319 cannot have been Sir William. Whatever the case, there was certainly a William de Lodelowe in the party attacking Isabel's house. Nor was he the only member of the family of that name.

The causes of the dispute which gave rise to the ejection of the elected bailiffs are obscure. They seem to have lain partly in factional rivalries within the town and partly in animosities amongst the county gentry, in particular between Richard de Harley and the Shropshire tenants of the Lestrange family who were among the group led by Isabel Borrey. But there was another striking feature of the affair. Isabel Borrey had, after her de Lodelowe husband's death, reverted to the name of her first husband. Aligned with her were her sons by Richard Borrey, Simon, Richard and John. In the attacking party were not only the William de Lodelowe, whose possible identity has been discussed above, but also her son by John de Lodelowe, Bogo de Lodelowe. He and John Borrey exchanged violent blows and the latter was one of the two men wounded. Why had this estrangement happened? At the time of his father's death in 1294/5 Bogo was too young to inherit his Campden estates, and in any case Isabel was the joint owner, so they would not have come to him until her death. Court records also reveal that there were disputes over John senior's will in which she and Laurence de Lodelowe, John's son by his earlier marriage, were involved.[77] It seems highly likely that the personal violence in which Bogo and John Borrey were involved was a sharp manifestation of this intra-family dispute over de Lodelowe money.

There was further and lethal violence yet to come. Isabel remained a wealthy and influential figure in Shrewsbury despite being fined for her part in the conspiracy to remove the bailiffs – she was Edward II's hostess when he came to Shrewsbury in 1322. On her death a few years after that (perhaps in 1325[78]) Bogo moved to secure his claim to the Campden estates, but before he could inherit he was murdered – by John Borrey. "The story finally ends in June 1327 when a royal pardon was issued by the king to John for the murder. The reason for the pardon is not given, but perhaps the enmity between the two men was recognised as having much wider and deeper roots than a sudden heated quarrel."[79]

Whether or not Sir William de Lodelowe was directly involved in these violent events, this is a fitting note upon which to end the account of his life, since it will recur in the career of his son, the second Laurence among the de Lodelowes of Stokesay.

CHAPTER 6

SIR LAURENCE DE LODELOWE

Very shortly after Sir William's death, his widow, Matilda, married William le Wynne. William's heir, Laurence, was sixteen when his father died. Consequently his lands were held in wardship until he came of age (of his larger properties Much Marcle by the king and Stokesay by his step father), and, because his mother was joint owner of the Hodnet estates with his de Lodelowe father, he did not succeed to those until his mother's death in 1347. This and the way that his estates were divided after his death strongly suggest that he used Stokesay as his family home. However by his twenties he was a well established figure in the county. He was called to arms under Oliver de Ingham to serve with the king in Scotland in 1322; in May 1324, already a knight, he was summoned to attend the Great Council at Westminster;[80] and in 1328 he attended the Parliament as knight of the shire.

The connection of the Stokesay de Lodelowes with national wool trade, which, at least so far as the public record reveals, had not been prominent in Sir William's time, reappears in the late 1330s. In 1337 Edward III secured a royal monopoly in the wool trade, under which he called directly upon the nation's wool to finance his war with France, the struggle which was to become known as the Hundred Years War. In 1337/38 30,000 sacks were to be collected – in the immediately following years the amount was less. The wool would be disposed of by the merchants, and the proceeds would be made available to the king as a loan. The collection of the wool was assigned to collectors by county with a target figure being set for them.[81] In Shropshire Laurence de Lodelowe was one of them. For in June 1339 an order was issued to reimburse Laurence de Lodelowe, William de Caynton and Richard de Weston, collectors of wool in Shropshire, for "what they shall be found on enquiry to have lost by the drying of wool detained in their custody for a long time unsacked for lack of canvas" and also "to have allowance for their labour and expenses in collecting that wool."[82]

This appointment was to bring trouble for Laurence. In August

1341 as 'supervisor of the king's wool' in Shropshire he was charged with delivering a quantity of wool to two citizens of Bordeaux who had been of service to the king. Laurence was dilatory in the discharge of this order, but he was not alone in this, since he and ten other men, who had been appointed on the previous 1st June, were in December ordered to be brought before the king and council for their failure to collect Shropshire's share of the wool which the king was that year levying from the country as a whole. Laurence appeared and successfully made representations that the amount demanded of him should be shared between himself and William de Caynton and Richard de Weston, his former colleagues as supervisors of the wool. "If they refuse to pay the wool and will not permit the arrest and sale of their goods, they are to be arrested by their bodies and incarcerated in the Tower of London as rebels." By 1st March 1342 Richard had discharged his debt and so, apparently, had William by the end of that month, for on 28th March the king appointed "John de Hampton to arrest, wherever found, Laurence de Lodelowe, one of the collectors appointed on 1st June last to levy the contingent in the county of Salop of the wool last granted to the king for the past year, who has borne himself negligently and contemptuously in the execution of divers writs of the king to him to hasten on the levy, whereby divers affairs which required a speedy levy of the wool remain unfinished to the king's damage and shame, and bring him before the king and council in Westminster to answer for the premises; and also to take into the king's hands all lands and goods which the said Laurence held at the day of his appointment, into whosesoever hands the same have come."[83] No further reference to this affair occurs, so it is to be presumed that Sir Laurence eventually came to heel. But the amount of wool involved was comparatively so small, 2 sacks and 8 stones (56 pounds) that his recalcitrance seems, even without full knowledge of all the circumstances, remarkable and suggests that he was of a somewhat high-handed character.

This supposition is given further credibility by the next recorded episode in his life. The sequence of events is not altogether clear from the record. Sir Laurence was indicted in Worcestershire for trespass by one John Wyard sometime in 1345. He failed to appear before the justices and was in consequence outlawed. He appealed to the king in September of that year to suspend the order, undertaking to appear for trial, and offering guarantors to that effect. On 27th September in the following year he was eventually outlawed for a violent assault upon John Wyard, but, since, according to Eyton, he had some years previously removed Stokesay and others of his properties from his own direct control by settling them in trust on other members of his family, the sheriff found none of his properties to confiscate. However, when his mother, Matilda – she was by now referred to as Maud -, died in 1347 the sheriff was able to distrain upon the lands he inherited from her (essentially the Hodnet estates). In April 1348 the king granted the goods and issues of the lands which had been confiscated from Sir Laurence to Laurence's son, John, but a month later, on 7th May, Sir Laurence was pardoned of his outlawry on the basis of a certificate from Chief Justice John de Stonore that he had surrendered to the Fleet Prison, and ultimately his estates were restored to him.[84] How the matter was resolved does not emerge but what is clear is that Sir Laurence was ready to operate on or beyond the very edges of the law.

This, in its turn, seems to have attracted reciprocated violence. In 1338 Laurence brought proceedings in three cases – one for theft from his property in Downton, another for an attack upon him in Ludlow and theft of goods worth 100 shillings, and a third for an attack upon his house in Ashford Bowdler, just south of Ludlow. This last case involved three men, one of whom was Richard de Mawardyn. Two years later Laurence's brother, William, was murdered at Worcester, Sir William de la Forde, on the first notice, being accused as the perpetrator. Sir William was outlawed, and in 1343 Sir Laurence brought an action against Sir John de Buildwas for harbouring the outlaw. But Sir William de la Forde was not alone in the murder, since in February 1344 pardon was granted to Richard de Mawardyn "for the death of William de Lodelowe, as well as for felonies, etc." Finally in May 1350 pardon was granted at the king's suit to John de Buildwas "for the receiving of William de la Forde and Richard de Mawardyn, lately indicted of the death of William de Lodelowe."[85] His brother Sir Laurence would also meet a violent end not long after.

Despite these skirmishes with the king and in his courts, Sir Laurence was still in these years entrusted with duties by the Crown, and it was not unusual that this should be so. In 1346, he was appointed as one of three commissioners in Shropshire to levy money from knight's fees to pay for the knighting of the king's eldest son, the Black Prince, surely a post which reflected well upon its holder.[86] And early in 1347, when the king, following upon his victory at Crécy, secured a levy of 20,000 sacks of wool in order to finance the campaign in France which led to the capture of Calais, the collectors of the 240 or so sacks apportioned to Shropshire were Roger Corbet of Caus, knight, Laurence de Lodelowe, knight, William de Leverset and Malcolm de Shenton.[87] Writing of "the ambivalent behaviour of the gentry themselves [in this period]", Nigel Saul observes "They had the ability to switch roles with apparently effortless ease. They appear first as poachers, then as gamekeepers; first as law-breakers, then as law-makers. In parliament they appeal for better enforcement of the law; back home they were the first to break it." To the list of country gentry whom Saul cites to support his case, he might well have added Sir Laurence de Lodelowe.[88]

However the final act of his life was one which gives him a special place in the history of the town of Ludlow. After the death of Laurence senior, his family maintained a presence and probably continued to live in Ludlow. In 1317 a lawsuit involved John, son of Laurence de Lodelowe, over a tenement in Ludlow. In 1323 William Orm, a Ludlow attorney brought an action against John, son of Laurence de Lodelowe. In the following year a John de Lodelowe was farmer of the rents of the Verdun part of the town, and the lay subsidy roll of 1327 placed John de Lodelowe tenth most well-to-do of the town's eighty two taxed inhabitants.[89] It may be supposed that he had the properties in the centre of town which his father Laurence had acquired in the 1280s and 1290s. Sir Laurence, also, held properties in Ludlow, but in a different part of the town, at the bottom of Corve Street on the west side by the lower Corve Gate. In 1350 he presented one of these properties to the Carmelite Friars, an inquisition in January of that year finding that there would be "no damage to the lord king if he grant to Laurence de Lodelowe chivaler that he may give one messuage in Lodelowe to the provincial prior of the Blessed Mary of Mount Carmel for a certain habitation for the friars of the Order there of a new building". On 10th February the king granted the Prior licence to proceed with the building "in consideration of 10s."[90]

What brought the Carmelites to Ludlow and what persuaded Sir Laurence de Lodelowe to his act of benefaction? The Order, the White Friars, was established in England in 1242, and by the end of that century there were twenty eight houses in the larger towns and cities around the country. The expansion of the Order slowed over the next years but the Carmelites were eager to establish themselves in the eighteen counties where there was no friary and in 1343 four further houses were sanctioned by the Pope. Ludlow was one of these. But before it could be built the Black Death engulfed the country in 1348 and 1349, sweeping away between a third and a half of the population. What its impact was on Ludlow is not known, but Michael Faraday cites "evidence of an unusual level of both death and charitable impulse among the propertied class" which "may reasonably be put down to the incidence of an unusual and frightening epidemic."[91] For the people and the church saw the devastating plague as divine retribution for man's sins. It is therefore reasonable to surmise, with Peter Klein, that Sir Laurence, having but recently escaped from the clutches of the criminal law, "in the spirit of the times sought to atone for his and mankind's sins by founding a Carmelite friary on his land in Ludlow."

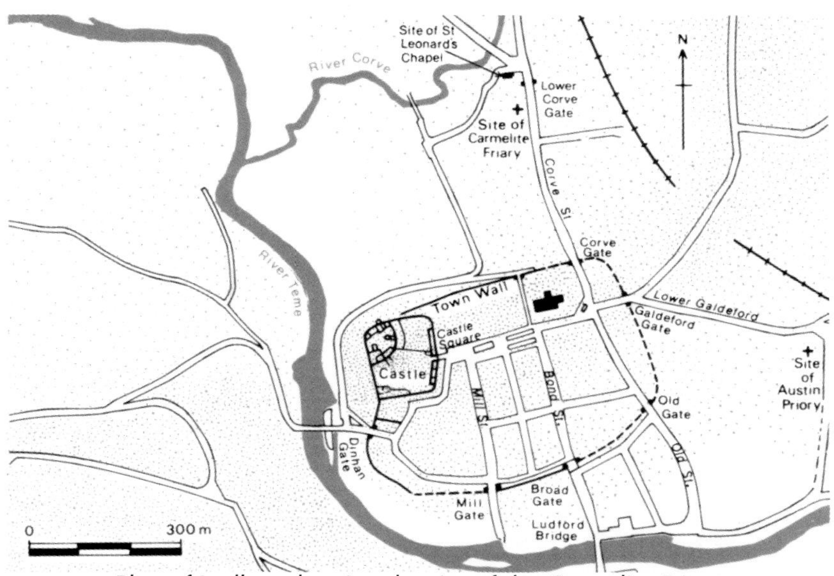

Plan of Ludlow showing the site of the Carmelite Friary.
From Klein and Roe, The Carmelite Friary, *1987.*

Soon after the royal grant of licence the friars moved into seven burgage plots, which Sir Laurence held of Joan Mortimer, countess of March, next door to the one on which they had permission to build. Relying, whether brazenly or in ignorance, on the strength of the royal licence for the single plot, they knocked down most of the buildings on the larger site and began work on constructing their church and other friary buildings, which were ready for occupation by 1352 and to be there for almost two hundred years. It was four years before the king became aware of this unlicensed encroachment, which caused the exchequer to lose half a mark (6 shillings and 8

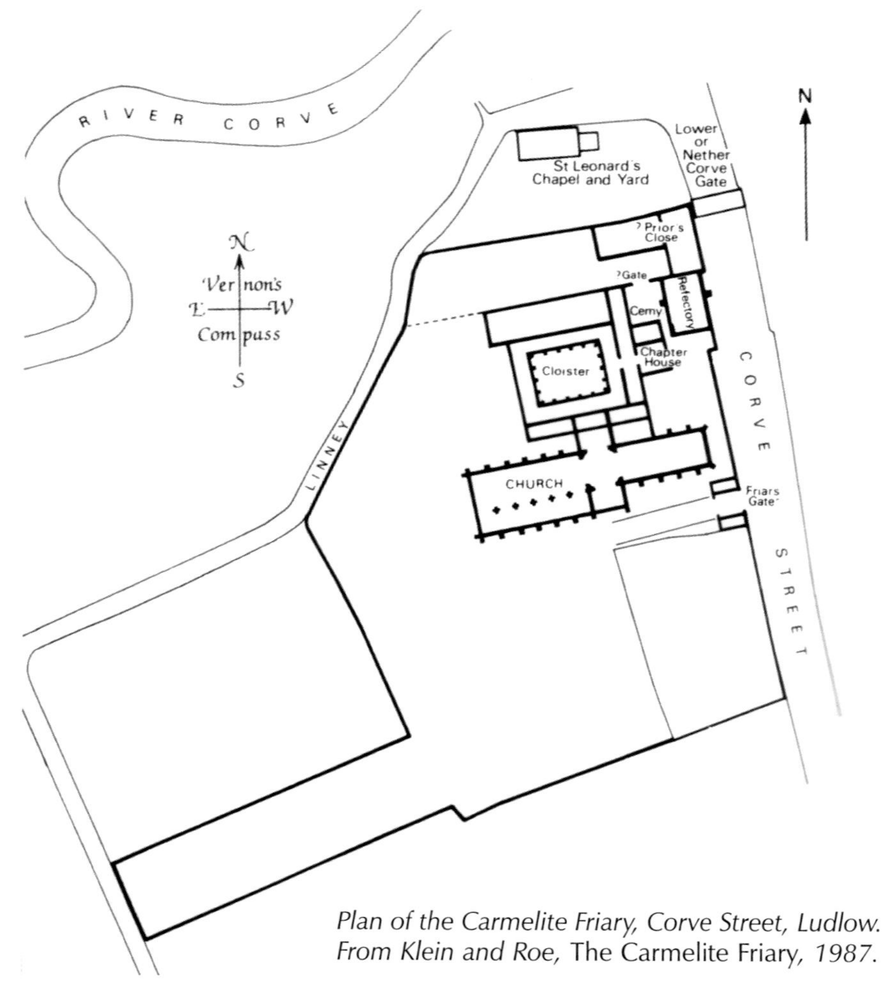

Plan of the Carmelite Friary, Corve Street, Ludlow. From Klein and Roe, The Carmelite Friary, *1987.*

pence) a year. The length of time it took the Crown to discover what had happened suggests that Sir Laurence may have connived at the friars' action, since he too would have lost income from it and, given his readiness to go to court in previous cases of trespass upon his property in Ludlow and elsewhere, would have alerted the king much sooner. There followed a commission of enquiry and in October 1355 the king held that "although the messuages...are forfeit to him, [he] has granted the same to the prior and friars that they may pray for the good estate of him, his consort and children and for their souls when they are dead, to hold for habitation by the services due."

By then Sir Laurence had been dead for two years. His death in Ludlow sometime in October or November 1353 (a different date is given in the three inquisitions *post mortem*) was sudden and he died intestate. In the Michaelmas term of 1354 a jury was called to enquire whether John de Haighton, William, son of John de Hopton, and Margaret, the widow of John de Hopton were guilty of his death, Hawise, Laurence's widow, having accused them. The prosecution was not immediately pursued; perhaps her indictment had not gone wide enough. For in May 1358 "pardon of special grace was given to Thomas de Hopton of the king's suit for the death of Laurence de Lodelowe, whereof he is indicted and appealed and of any consequent outlawry." This suggests that Sir Laurence's own actions were a contributory factor in his death, a suggestion which is confirmed by a "pardon of special grace to William, son of John de Hopton 'cangynot' of the king's suit for the death of Sir Laurence de Lodelowe, chivaler, whom he killed in self defence, as is said" given in 1361.[92] 'Cangynot' in the Patent Roll could be a corruption or misreading of Cangeford, Hopton Cangeford being a manor in Stanton Lacy, the Cangeford element appearing with various spellings elsewhere. The de Lodelowes had rented land in Stanton Lacy since 1296, so the affray in which Sir Laurence died may perhaps have arisen because of some dispute over the property there.[93]

However that may have been, the building of the chancel of the church in the Carmelite friary was sufficiently advanced to receive his body and he was buried in the sanctuary by John de Trillek, Bishop of Hereford on 19th November, whose register records "Memorandum that the Bishop buried Sir Laurence de Lodelowe, knight, in the Carmelite church at Ludlow and received and took away with him two horses, armour for two men, and 13s. and 6d., offerings made at the mass he then celebrated, without demur on the part of the friars." It was not however without demur of the rector of Ludlow, who promptly claimed that the bodies of all who died in the parish of St Laurence, Ludlow, should be brought to the church for a mass to be said over them, and that the offerings were properly his. The Bishop responded by directing the friars to "place a bier in the church as if for a funeral and...cause a mass to be celebrated for the soul of Sir Laurence de Lodelowe, and... permit the rector to take the offerings." Weyman believed that 'a tomb of alabaster grated with iron' which was recorded in the inventory of the friary at the time of its dissolution in 1538 was almost certainly the monument of Sir Laurence. However the tomb was found in the body of the church, and Klein argues that his tomb would have been placed only in the Quire.

So the life of Sir Laurence de Lodelowe came to what in some ways seems a tragi-comic end; with his body being laid to rest in the chapel which he intended to be the de Lodelowe family chapel and mausoleum in grounds which were unlawfully held; with a dispute between two distinguished clerics over the offerings given at his funeral mass; and with confusion still surrounding the circumstances of his death. It was of a piece with the turbulent years which had gone before.

Excavations at the Carmelite Friary, Ludlow, 1983-85.
From Klein and Roe, The Carmelite Friary, *1987.*

CHAPTER 7

LATER GENERATIONS

Sir Laurence's heir was his son, John, who was twenty six when his father died, so there were no problems of inheritance. Hawise, Laurence's widow, had held Stokesay, the de Lodelowe lands at Welbatch, at Westbury and at Roulton jointly with her husband, and when she remarried, sometime before 1357, her son, by now Sir John, settled on her for her lifetime all of the family's south Shropshire holdings.[94] Over the preceding fifty years these had grown substantially. In addition to the manor of Stokesay, Cold Weston, Overton and properties in Ludlow, they had acquired land in Stanton Lacy, Dodmore, Wigley, Felton, Downton, Steventon, Huntington, Ashford Bowdler and Greete, all close to Ludlow, and further afield at Clunbury in the Clun valley, and Corfton and Sparchford in Corvedale. In 1357 Sir John disposed of the property at Much Marcle to Roger de Mortimer, earl of March.[95] It seems likely therefore that since his father and mother had used Stokesay as the family home, Sir John had taken Hodnet as his base when he grew up and decided to remain there after his father's death, leaving his mother and her new husband, Nicholas of Moorhall, to live in, manage and have the benefit of the south Shropshire estate.

In his early manhood John served in the retinue of John Lestrange of Whitchurch in the campaign in France which culminated in the Battle of Crécy in 1346, and it was perhaps in consequence of his service in the French wars that he acquired his knighthood.[96] After he succeeded to the family estates, his career for the next thirty years until his death in 1382 followed closely the pattern of the landed gentry which his grandfather, Sir William, had established.

The Reverend J. B. Blakeway in his early nineteenth century work on the sheriffs of Shropshire stated that Sir John was sheriff from 1360 to 1362.[97] But, despite the fact that there had been a statutory requirement since 1340 that appointments should be annual, Richard, earl of Arundel, one of the great Shropshire magnates, had been sheriff since 1345 and continued to be so until his death in 1376, so Sir John's appointment was effectively to under-sheriff.

However after Arundel's death, "the commons of Shropshire regard[ing] the life shrievalty as having been to their great 'harm'", appointment became annual in Shropshire[98] and Sir John de Lodelowe was one of the first under the new dispensation, being appointed for 1379. It was a post of high responsibility and trust, with duties including the maintenance of the king's peace and the collection of certain of the royal revenues and acting as the official who carried out the orders of the Crown within his county. "Indeed no local-government policy could succeed without an efficient sheriff, for most royal writs and legal processes had to pass through his hands before they took effect." [99]

Sir John was elected knight of the shire to represent Shropshire in Parliament on six occasions between 1358 and 1377. He was present at the 'Good Parliament' of 1376, the best documented of all the medieval Parliaments, at which those who were held to have mismanaged the country in Edward III's last years, William Lord Latimer the Chamberlain, John Lord Neville the Steward and Alice Perrers, the king's mistress, were brought to book, and at which a number of significant constitutional changes were made, including the creation of a standing council. The Close Rolls record the expenses which he could claim from "the commons of the county, cities and boroughs excepted" for his attendance at Parliament at Westminster: for example, £6 8s. at 4s. a day for 16 days in 1366, £11 12s. for 29 days in 1374, and £28 for 70 days in 1377. He was collector of the poll tax in Shropshire in 1377; and in the same year he, with Nicholas Burnell, James de Audley, Roger Lestrange, Fulke Corbet and Roger de la Lee, was appointed by Edward III and subsequently by Richard II as commissioner of array in Shropshire in face of raids by the French and Castilians on the south coast of England and a growing fear of foreign invasion, being required "to array and equip all men in that county and to keep ever arrayed the men-at-arms and archers to resist foreign invasion…causing to be set up beacons in the usual places to give notice of the arrival of the enemy."[100]

Writing of Shropshire knights of the shire in the first half of the fourteenth century, the *Victoria County History of Shropshire* observed "A few men….were returned so often that they, at least, may be credited personally with the electors' confidence, and perhaps, from their accumulated experience, with personal standing in the

Commons." Referring to their experience of duties such as those performed by Sir John de Lodelowe, the *VCH* continued "In other words they were repeatedly recognised as suitable for high local office, not only by the local electors but by the government."[101] This judgment might be applied equally to Sir John, reflecting, no doubt, not merely his standing as a scion of a now well established and wealthy Shropshire gentry family but also his personal qualities as an administrator and public servant.

This sense of duty did not, however, extend to all aspects of his feudal obligations, as a pleasing case in the *De Banco Plea Rolls* of 1363 reveals. "John de Lodelowe, Kt. sued Ralph, earl of Stafford, for an illegal distress in his manor of Westbury...The Earl justified the distress on the ground that John held the manor of Westbury, of the Barony of Caus, by the service of hereditary cook at the Castle of Caus. The pleadings specified the service as attendance at the castle every Christmas Day, and standing at the kitchen dresser girded with an apron, and John refused to perform it. Judgment was given in favour of the Earl."[102]

Richard, Sir John's eldest son, was in his early twenties when his father died. His career of public service in Shropshire was to last for only three years, and in that respect was different from those of his longer lived fourteenth century forebears.[103] While he was making his way into public life, he joined enterprises led by two of Richard II's most powerful magnates and most influential opponents, the duke of Gloucester and the earl of Arundel, who, like Thomas of Lancaster in the reign of Edward II, first successfully defied the king and then were themselves brought down and executed. As his great grandfather Sir William had been eighty years before him, Sir Richard was associated with a winning cause while it was winning, but was dead by the time it was lost.

At his father's death he had already seen service in France from June 1380, when he was still in his teens, until March 1381, in an expedition led by Thomas of Woodstock, duke of Gloucester, one of the king's uncles, and under the command of Sir David Holgrave, a Worcestershire banneret, that is a knight able and entitled to bring his followers onto the field under his own banner. In the year after his father's death, with the king's licence, he gave possession of his Hodnet estates to a number of tenants, including Edmund de

Lodelowe, vicar of Wistanstow, whose advowson – that is the right to nominate the priest of the parish – the de Lodelowes had held from the beginning of the century, when Sir William acquired it for £40.[104] Edmund was almost certainly a member of the family, since others of that name had been vicars there in earlier days, including one of the first Laurence's sons, another Richard. And in subsequent years – the record is not clear when –Sir Richard similarly disposed the rest of his Shropshire lands and manors, one of the tenants being another de Lodelowe, Robert, who may perhaps be the Robert de Lodelowe recorded as sheriff of Shropshire in 1389. This arrangement, which, it may be supposed, generated annual revenue without the responsibility of direct management of the estate, perhaps reflected a decision on Richard's part at this time in his life to seek a career in a wider landscape than Shropshire could provide. Soon after these dispositions were made he was early in 1383 planning to go overseas, but this came to nothing. However in 1386 he was in the train of the earl of Stafford, his overlord at Westbury, on a pilgrimage to Jerusalem, being a witness to the earl's will which was made in Rhodes in the September of that year. And a year later he was serving in the personal retinue of the earl of Arundel, another of the greatest magnates in the land, himself with substantial Shropshire estates and of paramount influence in the county,[105] and at that time the admiral of the naval force deployed to patrol the Channel that summer against French raids.

By this time he was knighted. In the last years of his life the focus of his activities was turning more towards Shropshire. He was given an *ad hoc* commission in 1387 to enquire into the king's affairs in relation to Wenlock Priory – a commission which, three years later and less than a month before his death, being faced with prosecution for dereliction of duty, he was required to declare on oath in chancery had never been delivered to him, perhaps because at the time he was on service with the earl of Arundel.[106] He was elected to the Parliament of 1388, the so-called Merciless Parliament in which the two great men with whom his career had already been associated, the duke of Gloucester and the earl of Arundel, together with the earl of Warwick, known as 'The Appellants', secured the conviction for treason of five of the king's leading friends. It may have been through the influence of Arundel that Sir Richard obtained his place, and he was elected twice again in 1390. He was appointed justice of the peace in Shropshire in July 1388, in company with the earl of Arundel, Nicholas de Audley, Hugh de Burnell, Richard Talbot, John Lestrange, Robert de Charlton, Richard Corbet, John Hull, Thomas Newport and Thomas de la Lee, but in the following year, the king, having recovered control of the government and dismissed Arundel, appointed a fresh and almost completely different commission which did not contain Sir Richard.[107] He became entangled in 1390 in a violent dispute over some of the Corbet estates, and he was at odds with his de Lodelowe relative, Edmund, over the latter's occupation of the Wistanstow living. Before that suit could be settled Richard was dead, at the age of 29. As he had not married, his estate was inherited by his brother John.

The second Sir John in the direct line has left little trace in the historical record. His importance in the Ludlow story lies beyond his lifetime through his marriage to Isabel, daughter of Sir Ralph Lingen of Wigmore, the last of whose husbands (she had three) was Sir Fulke de Pembridge, the lord of Tong in east Shropshire. In 1410 Isabel obtained royal licence to establish Tong College and the Collegiate

The collegiate church of St. Bartholemew in Tong, founded by Isabel de Pembridge in 1410. (Photograph by Dr John Leonard.)

church of St Bartholomew in Tong. The College was to have five chaplains among whose duties, typically of religious foundations at this time, was the care of thirteen paupers who lived in the associated almshouses; they were also "to pray for the good estate of the king and Thomas Beaufort his brother and the said Isabel and for their souls after death and the souls of the king's progenitors, the said Fulk [de Pembridge] and Margaret sometime his wife, Thomas Peytevyne, 'chivaler' [Isabel's first husband], John Ludlowe, 'chivaler' and the parents and ancestors of the said Isabel."[108] One of Sir John's and Isabel's daughters, Benedicta, married Sir Richard Vernon of Haddon Hall in Derbyshire, a nephew of Sir Fulke de Pembridge, speaker of the Parliament in 1426 and treasurer of Calais between 1444 and 1450, and Sir John's son and heir, William, married Isabel, Sir Richard's sister. This consolidated a connection with the Vernon family which, three generations later, was to inherit the de Lodelowe estates. Isabel and Benedicta are the first in the family line to have surviving memorials, which are to be found among the superb collection of monuments in Tong church.[109] Sir John had died in 1398, his male heir being William, aged then 'one and a quarter and more'.[110] Isabel de Pembridge, having held their estates jointly with her husband, continued in them until her death in 1447.[111]

The monument of Sir Fulke and Isabel de Pembridge in St. Bartholomew's Church, Tong. (Photograph by Dr John Leonard.)

William and his son Richard span the fifteenth century.[112] The years of William's childhood and adolescence saw the Lancastrian Henry IV's usurpation of the throne, the northern rebellion of the Percys which culminated in the Battle of Shrewsbury and the insurrection of Owain Glyn Dwr, the latter two of which were very close to home. There is no indication in the records of how they impinged upon the family's fortunes. However as soon as William came to manhood, he quickly found a place among the most active members of the Shropshire governing gentry. He was knight of the shire only once, in 1427, in contrast to the Parliamentary career of his grandfather, the first Sir John, and in 1450, he was appointed collector of taxes for Shropshire, but his service in the administration of justice in the county, both as a law enforcement officer and on the judicial bench, lasted for more than forty years. He was sheriff six times between 1418[113] and 1448 and appointed to the peace commission for Shropshire on twenty two occasions between 1420 and 1469. Until 1449 he was not regularly a justice of the peace, being on only six of the twenty four commissions between 1420 and 1441, but from 1449 onwards until 1469 he was on all sixteen.[114]

The *Victoria County History of Shropshire* says that "[Richard, duke of] York's emergence as a political force in the 1450s was not of a kind to give him much influence over the Shropshire peace commission, whose predominantly Lancastrian character was not altered until 1460."[115] But if one takes into account the de Lodelowe's origins in and associations with the town of Ludlow, one of the principal seats of the earls of March (now the dukes of York), their earlier sale of their Herefordshire property to the earl of March, William's numerous properties in south Shropshire and his continuous service on the peace commission after Edward IV (the son of Richard, duke of York) had seized the throne (he was one of only three men to be present on all of the commissions from 1453 to 1469), William's Yorkist sympathies and connections must be acknowledged. This attachment is confirmed in another way. A royal commission of 12th August 1461, five months after Edward IV had taken the throne in the previous March, "to the king's kinsman, Richard earl of Warwick, William earl of Arundel, John Audley of Audley...." required them and others, including William Ludlowe, "to urge the king's subjects of the county of Salop to array a force at their own expense for defence of the county and the adjoining parts of Wales against the rebels, to be at Hereford on the Nativity of the Virgin [8th September]".[116] And yet his earlier career, especially as sheriff, suggests that he must also have had the confidence of the Lancastrian supporters in the county, notably the Talbots, the earls of Shrewsbury, together with the Yorks, the greatest magnates in Shropshire from the 1430s.[117]

Official documents referred to William, if they gave him a rank at all, as 'esquire', never as 'knight', even in lists where others were so designated, and indeed in the royal licence which enabled him to take final possession of his estates on his mother's death in 1447, he was called "the king's esquire, William Ludlowe, son and heir of John Ludlowe, knight".[118] So, although a knight of the shire as a Parliamentary representative of the county, he was not formally raised to the knighthood as his fourteenth century ancestors had been and as his son, Richard, was in the year after his father's death. In a deed relating to a property transaction in Westbury in 1449 he was named as 'William Ludlowe of Stokesay esquire'[119], and that, together with the likelihood that his widowed mother Isabel remained at Hodnet, with her strong interests at Tong relatively nearby, and evidence of William's involvement with properties in Ludlow, suggests that for the first time since Sir Laurence's day, Stokesay was the principal home of the family.

William's son Richard formally succeeded to his father's estates in October 1474 at the age of thirty. He had been appointed constable of Caus Castle by the gift of Humphrey, duke of Buckingham, in 1452. Otherwise what his career was before then is uncertain. But it is significant that when Edward IV's son was created Edward Prince of Wales on 18th April 1475, Richard Ludlow was present in Saint Edward's Chamber at Westminster, as a Knight of the Bath created on that day.[120] This may have been in recognition of his father's long service to the Crown in Shropshire, but, as that had never been formally rewarded, it seems more likely that Sir Richard was created on his own merits, perhaps for active service in the Yorkist cause at and before the battle of Tewksbury in 1471 when Edward IV finally secured the Crown. He was also present with the dukes, earls, lords and knights (some ninety of them) at the coronation of Richard III on 6th July 1483.[121] Sir Richard himself followed in his father's footsteps in the administration of justice in Shropshire. He held the office of sheriff twice, in 1478 and in 1490, and was appointed justice of the peace on fourteen occasions between 1475 and 1495.[122] In his biography in the *History of Parliament* he is recorded as representing Shropshire in 1485-6, and possibly on four other occasions in 1483 and 1484.

When he died in 1498, there were no males in the direct line to succeed him, his son, Sir John, and his grandson, John, having predeceased him. His estates passed to two granddaughters, both of whom had married into the Vernon family in 1497. Ann Ludlow, who was seventeen, married Thomas Vernon, third son of Sir Henry Vernon of Tong Castle and Haddon Hall, and Alice Ludlow, who was fifteen, married Humphrey, the fourth son. Sir Henry Vernon was the grandson of Sir Richard Vernon who had married Benedicta de Lodelowe, so the two branches of the family were reunited two generations on. The Stokesay estates passed to Ann and Hodnet to Alice.[123] The Ludlow name which Laurence had established at Stokesay over two hundred years before was now part of the Castle's history.

The monument of Sir Richard Vernon and Bendicta de Ludlow in St. Bartholemew's Chuch, Tong. (Photograph by Dr John Leonard.)

CHAPTER 8

THE HERITAGE

Although the association of the name Ludlow with Stokesay ended with the death of Sir Richard in 1498, the memories of the Stokesay Ludlows lingered on in the town itself well into the sixteenth century, the Bailiff's accounts for 1560 recording rentals for properties in Castle Street and the Narrows (King Street) which belonged to the heirs of Ludlow, lord of Stoke, and of a burgage in Corve Street outside the gate 'of the lords of Stoke, sometime William Ludlow'. And Ludlows remained among the gentry names of Shropshire for several generations longer, the Ludlows of the Morehouse at Shipton in Corvedale, being descendants in a junior branch of the Stokesay family (a Laurence Ludlow's memorial is in the church there). The family connection with Hodnet, through Alice Ludlow's marriage to Humphrey Vernon, was passed on by the last of the Vernons, Miss Henrietta Vernon, on her death in 1752, to a second cousin who was married to Thomas Heber, a member of a West Yorkshire family. In the nineteenth century that family became the Heber-Percys, when a Heber daughter married a nephew of the duke of Northumberland and the Heber-Percys retain the estate to the present day. There was to be no such unbroken line of inheritance at Stokesay. There, the last of the Vernons, descended from Ann Ludlow, sold the manor to Sir George Mainwairing in 1598. He sold it on to the Craven family in 1620 in whose possession, as absentee landlords, it remained until it was bought by J. D. Allcroft in 1869. In 1992 the Castle came into the guardianship of English Heritage.

Tong College passed into private hands in 1546 at the dissolution of the monasteries and its buildings, which were in an advanced state of dilapidation by the mid-eighteenth century, have now entirely disappeared. Between 1538 and 1542 the Carmelite Friary in Ludlow was acquired by Thomas Vernon and was rapidly demolished – Vernon claiming it and its contents "as his ancestors were the founders, and there is such an ill rule kept [there]".[124] The Victorian chapel of St Leonard, which is now used as a printers, stands upon the site.

The gate into the site of the Carmelite Friary in Corve Street, Ludlow.
St. Leonard's Chapel, behind, now a printers, dates from the 19th century.

The Vernon monuments in Tong church recall the later days of the Ludlow family, but of the family's buildings and residences Stokesay Castle alone remains. It had been the home for over two hundred years of a family who through eight generations had served their county and, in some instances, their country with great distinction. And the Castle of itself bears eloquent witness to the business acumen and the national prestige of the men who had founded that family's fortune, Nicholas and Laurence de Lodelowe. An inscription in the house of a Lancashire wool merchant, John Barton, is said to have borne the message: "I thanke God and ever shall/ It is the sheepe hath payed for all."[125] One could scarcely find a more appropriate inscription to place over the fireplace in the solar at Stokesay.

Stokesay Castle from the south west.

A Note on Sources

The principal sources used for this account are the following:

The Calendars of State Papers: Calendars of Patent Rolls (CPR), Calendars of Close Rolls (CCR) and Calendars of Fine Rolls (CCR) – and Calendars of Inquisitions *post mortem* (IPM). All of these are available at the Public Record Office (PRO) and, locally, at Shropshire Archives (SA).

Transcripts of original documents – King's Bench, De Banco Rolls, Feet of Fines, Coram Rege Rolls, Justices Itinerant Rolls and the Muniments of Title of the Palmers' Gild of Ludlow – made by Michael Faraday, a set being given by him to the Ludlow Historical Research Group (LHRG). The Palmers' Gild documents are to be found among the Ludlow Borough collection at Shropshire Archives (LB 5/2 series) and in the LHRG collection at the Ludlow Museum and Library Resource Centre.

Volumes 4 to 7 of *The Oxford History of England* give the detailed historical context for the lives of the Stokesay Ludlows, and Miri Rubin's *The Hollow Crown A History of Britain in the Late Middle Ages*, Allen Lane 2005, provides an informative account for the non-specialist. Michael Faraday's *Ludlow 1085 – 1660*, Dorothy Cromarty's *Everyday Life in Medieval Shrewsbury* and Dorothy and Robert Cromarty's *The Wealth of Shrewsbury in the early fourteenth century* for Ludlow and Shrewsbury respectively, and the Reverend R. W. Eyton's *The Antiquities of Shropshire* for the county as a whole place them in their local setting. *The Victoria County History of Shropshire*, Vol. III, OUP 1979 (VCH) deals with the government of Shropshire in the period.

The medieval wool trade in England is described by Eileen Power in *The Wool Trade in Medieval History* and by T. H. Lloyd in *The English Wool Trade in the Middle Ages*.

The Transactions of the Shropshire Archaeological and Historical Society (TSAS) – available at Shropshire Archives and at the Ludlow Museum and Resource Centre - are an indispensable source for lists of members of the Shrewsbury Merchants Gild, and Shrewsbury and Shropshire Members of Parliament.

Endnotes

Chapter 2

1 For a full account of this period in Ludlow's history see Faraday M. A., *Ludlow 1085 – 1660*, Phillimore, 1991.
2 Train C. J., *The Walls and Gates of Ludlow*, Ludlow Historical Research Group, 1999, pp. 20 – 25.
3 Ibid., ch. 3, quoting Davies R. R., *Lordship and Society in the March of Wales 1282 – 1400*, pp. 66-7.
4 Power E., *The Wool Trade in English Medieval History*, OUP 1941, p.21.
5 Ibid., p. 47.

Chapter 3

6 Reaney P. H., *The Origin of English Surnames*, London 1967, pp. 314f.
7 It was not until the fifteenth century that the plain form of the surname – Lodelowe or Ludlowe and finally Ludlow - began to be regularly used. I have employed the conventional usage of the time.
8 *The Register of Thomas de Cantilupe, Bishop of Hereford 1275 -1282*, Hereford 1906.
9 Cromarty D., *Everyday Life in Medieval Shrewsbury*, Shropshire Books, 1991, p. 26.
10 *CPR Edward I 1272 – 1281*, pp. 23, 24, 67.
11 SA LB 5/2/331.
12 SA LB5/2/336.
13 *CPR Edward I 1272 – 1281*, p. 325.
14 Drinkwater C. H. , 'The Merchant Gild of Shrewsbury: Seven Rolls of the Thirteenth Century', *TSAS, 2nd Series Vol. XII*, pp. 229ff.
15 I am grateful to Bill Champion for permission to quote from his *Notes on 1 – 3 Pride Hill Shrewsbury, including 'Bennett's Hall' (2 – 3 Pride Hill)*, 2000, unpublished.
16 For a discussion of these developments see Lloyd T. H., *The English Wool Trade in the Middle Ages*, CUP 1977.
17 *Calendar of Chancery Rolls Supplementary 1277 – 1326*, pp1f.
18 *CPR Edward I 1272 – 1281*, pp. 247 and 256.
19 PRO, KB 26/146, m.2v.
20 *CPR Henry III 1266 – 1272*, p. 688.
21 Burton J. 'The Cistercian Adventure' in *The Cistercian Abbeys of Britain*, ed. Robinson D., Batsford 1998, p. 28.
22 *CCR Edward I 1279 – 1288*, p. 424.
23 PRO, *De Banco Rolls*, CP40/53, m.10r.
24 *CPR Edward I 1272 – 1281*, pp. 256 and 325.
25 Drinkwater, op. cit.

Chapter 4

26 Faraday, op. cit. pp. 143f.

27 *The Register of Thomas de Cantilupe*, op. cit., p. 120.

28 Drinkwater C. H., 'The Merchant Gild of Shrewsbury' *TSAS, 2nd Series Vol. II* pp. 36ff.

29 Cromarty D. and R., *The Wealth of Shrewsbury in the Early Fourteenth Century*, Shropshire Archaeological and Historical Society, 1993, p. 55, suggest that John de Lodelowe perished with his brother, Laurence (see p. 27). Although none of the three contemporary accounts record this specifically, the Dunstable Annalist (*Annales Monastici* Vol. III, pp. 389f) states that the king's clerk and "*unus ditissimus mercator*" perished with Laurence. The "very rich merchant" could have been John, although it seems strange that he should not have been named in circumstances which involved his brother's death. Both the inquisition *post mortem* on John and the order to the escheator to take into the king's hands the lands he held in chief (*CFR Edward I 1272 – 1307,* p. 395) are dated August 1295. The delay since November 1294 was considerable, and on the assumption that John died with Laurence, who was on royal business and whose death was reported to the court immediately, one would have supposed that the authorities would have moved sooner to seize John's lands for the benefit of the king. However, official action could have been delayed for some reason, so that argument is not conclusive. Nonetheless the evidence does point to John's dying sometime in 1295 rather than with his brother.

30 Whitfield C., *A History of Chipping Campden*, 1958, pp. 40ff. The date of John's burial is wrongly given as 1286.

31 Burke J., *A Genealogical and Heraldic History of the Commons of Great Britain and Ireland*, Vol. I, 1833, pp. 32ff.

32 PRO *Feet of Fines* CP 25(1)/193/6, No. 16.

33 SA LB 8/1/2.

34 PRO KB 27/37.

35 *Select Bills in Eyre of Shropshire*, Selden Society, 20 Edward I.

36 *Calendar of Chancery Rolls Supplementary 1277 – 1326*, p. 2.

37 PRO *Justices Itinerant Rolls*, Just. 1/739m.3f. "Laurence de Lodelowe and others in Ludlow sold cloth against the assize and so are in mercy."

38 Cromarty D. and R., op. cit., p. 54.

39 These figures have been assembled from a variety of sources – the *Calendar of Close Rolls* from 1280 onwards, the *De Banco Rolls* and the *Justices Itinerant Rolls*, and Ludlow references excerpted by Michael Faraday and lodged with the Ludlow Historical Research Group.

40 *CCR Edward I 1302 – 1397*, p. 493.

41 Eyton R. W., *The Antiquities of Shropshire*, London 1853 – 1860, Vol. I, p. 68.

42 *Calendars of Inquisitions post mortem Edward I 1272 – 1309*, p. 395 and

Edward II 1307 – 1327, p. 34.
43 Eyton, op. cit., Vol. V, p. 36.
44 *Calendar of Charter Rolls Henry III – Edward I 1259 – 1300*, p. 255.
45 *CPR Edward I 1281 – 1292*, p. 450. The discussion of the building history of Stokesay Castle is based upon Munby J., *Stokesay Castle*, English Heritage, 1993, Mercer E., *English Architecture to 1900: The Shropshire Experience*, Logaston Press 2003, and Moran M., *Vernacular Buildings of Shropshire*, Logaston Press, 2003.
46 Train, op. cit., p. 19.
47 Lloyd, op. cit., pp. 76ff. and *Annales Monastici*, Vol. III, Annales de Dunstaplia, pp. 389f.
48 *CPR Edward I 1292 – 1301*, p. 99 and *CCR Edward I 1288 – 1296*, p. 360.
49 PRO E159/mb 68.
50 *Annales Monastici*, Vol. IV, Annales de Wigornia, p. 518.
51 *Calendar of Chancery Warrants 1244 – 1326*, p. 54.
52 Munby, op. cit. p. 1, quoting the Victorian authors Turner and Parker.

Chapter 5
53 Lloyd, op. cit., pp. 90 and 133. PRO *De Banco Rolls*, CP 40/109, m. 47v.
54 *The Shropshire Lay Subsidy of 1327*, ed. Rev. W. G. D. Fletcher, Oswestry, 1907, reprinted from TSAS, p. 154.
55 The inquisition *post mortem* on his death in 1316 gives an account of his properties (*Calendar of Inquisitions post mortem, Edward II, Vol. V*, pp. 33 and 34).
56 Weyman H. T. in *TSAS, 4th Series, Vol. X*, p. 22.
57 *CPR Edward II 1307 – 1313*, pp. 29 and 31.
58 See the indexes to the *Calendars of Patent Rolls* for these years for the details.
59 *The Parliamentary Writs and Writs of Military Summons, Vol II , Abstract and Calendar Division I*, ed. F. Palgrave, 1830 for 1311 and 1314 and *CPR Edward II 1313 – 1317*, pp. 351f. for 1316.
60 Shaw W. A., *The Knights of England*, Vol. II, 1906 and Moore Rev. C., *The Knights of Edward I*, Vol. III, 1930.
61 *CPR Edward II 1313 – 1317*, pp. 21 and 23.
62 I am grateful to Bob Cromarty for this information.
63 PRO *De Banco Rolls*, CP 40/115, m.10r.
64 Cromarty D. and R., op. cit., p. 55.
65 Ibid. pp. 107 and 109.
66 Lloyd, op. cit., p. 133. Lloyd refers to him as Laurence's brother, but that was John de Lodelowe senior who was already dead.
67 *Calendar of Chancery Warrants 1244 – 1326*, January 9th, 1302, p. 153.
68 *CCR Edward I 1302 – 1307*, p. 255.
69 SA *Calendar of Deeds and Charters, Vol. IV*, 3727 and 3728.

70 Ibid., 3731 and 3732 refer to property transactions in Shrewsbury by John de Lodelowe, son and heir of Thomas de Lodelowe, knight, in the early 1360s; that Sir Thomas de Lodelowe very probably being the Thomas de Lodelowe who represented Shrewsbury in the Parliaments of 1346 and 1348.
71 OED definition.
72 A full account of these events may be found in Dorothy Cromarty's *Everyday Life in Medieval Shrewsbury*, pp 91-94 and in the Cromartys' article 'The Shrewsbury Town Riot of 1303' in *TSAS Vol. LXXIII* 1998, pp. 13ff.
73 Cromarty D. and R., op. cit., pp. 89 and 103.
74 *CPR Edward II 1307 – 1313*, p. 487.
75 Ibid., p. 423.
76 Weyman, op. cit., p. 22.
77 PRO *De Banco Rolls* CP40/115, m. 10r (1296/7) and *Coram Rege Rolls*, KB27/150, m.22d (1297).
78 Cromarty D. and R., op. cit. p. 55.
79 Cromarty D., op. cit., p. 95.

Chapter 6
80 Moore Rev. C., op.cit.
81 See Lloyd, op. cit., chapter 5 'Edward III – woolmonger extraordinary' for a full account.
82 *CCR Edward III 1339 – 1341*, pp 169f.
83 *CCR Edward III 1341 – 1343*, pp. 205f.; *CFR Edward III 1337 – 1347*, pp. 254f; *CPR Edward III, 1340 – 1343*, pp. 368, 445f., and 422f.
84 Eyton, op. cit., Vol. V, p. 59 and *CPR Edward III 1348 – 1350*, pp. 85 and 90.
85 PRO *Coram Rege Rolls*, KB 27/310, m.11b., KB 27/318 Rex m.3a., KB 27/330 Rex 7a., and *CPR Edward III 1343 – 1345*, p. 214 and *CPR Edward III 1348 – 1350*, p. 502.
86 *CFR Edward III 1337 – 1347*, pp. 490 and 492.
87 Lloyd, op. cit., p. 200 and *CFR Edward III 1347 – 1356*, p. 5.
88 Saul N., 'Conflict and Consensus in English Local Society' in *Politics and Crisis in Fourteenth Century England*, ed. Taylor and Childs, Gloucester, 1990, p. 40.
89 PRO *Justices Itinerant Rolls* Just. 1/1366, m. 49d., PRO *De Banco Rolls* CP40/247 m. 75r., Faraday, op. cit. p. 26, and *Shropshire Lay Subsidy Roll of 1327*, op.cit., p. 290.
90 This section is largely based upon *The Carmelite Friary, Corve Street, Ludlow: Its History and Excavation*, by P. Klein and A. Roe, published in 1987 as Research Paper Number 6 in the Ludlow Historical Research Group Series. I am grateful to Peter Klein for permission to reproduce illustrations from this.

91 Faraday, op. cit., p. 160.
92 PRO *Coram Rege Rolls*, KB 27/377 Rex m.98 and Rex 27b, *CCR Edward III 1354 – 1360*, p. 629 and CPR Edward III 1361 – 1364, p.16.
93 PRO *Feet of Fines* CP25 (1)/194/7.

Chapter 7

94 PRO *Feet of Fines* CP25 (1)/195/15.
95 *CPR Edward III 1354 – 1358*, p. 584.
96 Weyman, op. cit., p. 179.
97 Blakeway, Rev. J. B., *The Sheriffs of Shropshire with their Armorial Bearings*, 1831.
98 *VCH Vol. III*, p. 74.
99 Ibid. p. 75.
100 *CPR Richard II 1377 – 1385*, p. 40.
101 *VCH Vol. III*, p. 235.
102 *Pedigrees from Plea Rolls 1200 – 1500*, ed. Wrottesley, p. 91.
103 Much of the following account derives from *The House of Commons 1386 – 1421, Vol. III, Members E – O*, History of Parliament Trust 1992, p. 650.
104 Eyton, op. cit. Vol. XI, p. 362.
105 *VCH Vol. III*, pp. 54ff.
106 *CPR Richard II 1385 – 1389*, p. 388 and *CCR Richard II 1389 -1392*, p. 303.
107 *CPR Richard II 1388 – 92*, pp. 137 and 342.
108 *CPR Henry IV 1408 – 1413*, p. 280.
109 See Auden, Rev. J. E., 'Documents relating to Tong College', *TSAS Series 3, Vol. VIII*, pp. 169ff. for the relevant pedigrees.
110 *Calendar of Inquisitions post mortem Richard II 1377 – 1399*, pp. 426f.
111 *CPR Henry VI 1446 – 1452*, p. 51.
112 There is a point of obscurity in relation to the family at this period. In the Inquisition *post mortem* on Sir Fulke's death in 1409 a William Luddelow (sic) and his wife, Isabel, were mentioned and they were named again in the licence to establish Tong College a year later. The Tong licence indicates that Isabel was the sister of Sir Richard Vernon, but was this William Lodelowe the son and heir of Sir John de Lodelowe by Isabel de Pembridge? 1409 might seem rather early for William, son of Sir John, to have been married (if the age given in the inquisition *post mortem* of his father is correct, he would have been little more than 13), but youthful marriages for dynastic reasons were not uncommon. Some Victorian genealogies stated that when William de Lodelowe was appointed sheriff of Shropshire for 1418 he was designated 'knight' while later references to William de Lodelowe call him 'esquire' (see, for example, Morris G., *Shropshire Genealogies Vol. III*, pp. 195ff and *Vol. V*, p. 77, SA 6001/2790 and /2792). They therefore suggested that the latter

must have been a second and younger William de Lodelowe. Morris speculated that he was Sir William's son. This cannot be right, since on Isabel de Pembridge's death in 1447 the properties which she had held in dower descended to "William de Lodelowe esquire, son and heir of John Ludelowe" (*CPR Henry VI 1446 – 1452*, p.51). Furthermore, although a list of High Sheriffs of the County of Shropshire dated 1771 (SA6001/6857) gives a William Ludlowe as sheriff in 1416 [sic] and designates him 'knight', in the Patent Roll for the appointment of the 1418 sheriff he was not so designated, although a number of other sheriffs were. It should, however, be noted that William, son of Sir John, would have been only 22 when he took office as sheriff, substantially younger than others who held the office around this time and whose ages can be estimated; but again that is not conclusive. There being two William de Lodelowes active in Shropshire administration in these decades and referred to in the public records without differentiation might be thought unlikely. The balance of evidence and argument points towards a single William de Lodelowe, son of Sir John and husband of Isabel Vernon, whose public career ran from 1418 onwards.

113 But see endnote 112 above.

114 *List of Sheriffs for England and Wales from the earliest times to A.D. 1831*, Lists and Indexes No. IX, HMSO 1963, and CPR Appendices of Peace Commissions over the period.

115 *VCH, Vol. III*, p. 57.

116 *CPR Edward IV 1461 – 1467*, p. 98.

117 *VCH*, ibid.

118 *CPR Henry VI 1446 – 1452*, p. 51.

119 SA 6000/9344.

120 Shaw W. A., *The Knights of England, Vol. II*, London 1906, p. 113.

121 *The Coronation of Richard III: the extant documents*, ed. Sutton and Hammond, Gloucester 1983.

122 *List of Sheriffs*, op. cit., and *CPR*, relevant appendices.

Chapter 8

123 *Calendar of Inquisitions post mortem Henry VII, Vol. II*, pp. 77ff.

124 Klein, op. cit. p. 19.

125 Simon Jenkins, *England's Thousand Best Churches*, The Penguin Press, 1999, p. 520.

INDEX